A model for evaluating quality of care provided, and quality of life experienced, in residential care homes for elderly people

HOMES ARE FOR **LIVING** IN

Produced by a project team comprising members of the Social Services Inspectorate in the North West and of the Social Services Departments of **Cheshire, Lancashire, Liverpool, Salford, St Helens and Tameside**

London: HMSO

First published 1989
Sixth impression 1996

ISBN 0 11 321229 1

FOREWORD

By Lady Wagner OBE, PhD

Chair of the Report of the
Independent Review of
Residential Care

It is most encouraging to know that the Social Services Inspectorate, along with many other individuals and agencies concerned with providing and regulating residential care, believe that homes have a mission which goes beyond merely housing people and keeping them clean, safe and well nourished. They believe that homes are, indeed, for *living* in. Life in them should be a positive experience in which residents are enabled to do *more*, not less, with their lives; to exercise *more*, not less control and choice; to live in *dignity* and *privacy*; and to have their *basic human rights* safeguarded. That was the message and those were the principles upon which 'A Positive Choice', the report of the Independent Review of Residential Care, based its recommendations.

These aspirations underpin this publication. The papers in it form a model to use for evaluating that most elusive of concepts, namely quality of life experience. The model is concerned with changing the way we look at homes and changing the language we use to describe what we see. It contains mechanisms for collecting and organising information so as to enable users to evaluate what *is* in relation to clearly articulated notions of what *ought to be*. These notions are derived from basic values which I am sure most of us would hold dear, such as the importance of personal privacy and confidentiality of information.

The model has been produced as a result of collaboration between Social Services Inspectors and representatives of six Social Services Departments in the North West and is based on practical experience. The fact that three private homes and a voluntary home as well as local authority homes were used in evaluating the model is particularly pleasing. Those involved with the production of the model should be encouraged that a private home owner proposes to use it as an internal training manual.

I am sure the model will provide a most valuable contribution towards a future response by the Department of Health to the Report of the Independent Review of Residential Care. I hope that it will be a useful tool for all those involved in residential care, whether they be owners, managers, practitioners, trainers, inspectors or service consumers.

PROJECT TEAM

Department of Health Social Services Inspectorate North Western Region	**David Carrington*** **Margaret Clough*** **Maire Gibson*** **Robin Hughes*** **Peter Munro*** **Jennifer Acheson (Secretary)**
Cheshire Social Services Department	**Sue Lightup*** **Pam Smith** **Geoff Sykes**
Lancashire Social Services Department	**David Charnley*** **Alan Jefferson** **Joyce Thom**
Liverpool Social Services Department	**Jackie Daniels** **Maria Wrigley***
Salford Social Services Department	**Vivienne Hare***
St Helens Social Services Department	**Geoff Brown*** **Carole Elford**
Tameside Social Services Department	**Marion Bowden***

Note: Those marked * will respond to enquiries regarding experience in using the model. Local authority team members can be contacted at the headquarters offices of their departments.

CONTENTS

SETTING THE SCENE

Introduction

During recent years there has been increasing public concern about the quality of care provided for elderly people in residential care homes in both local authority and independent sectors. Specific concern has been expressed by individuals, agencies, professional bodies and other organisations that methods of monitoring and developing standards in homes were inadequate or inappropriate.

Much of the debate has focused on responsibilities and procedures, such as who should inspect and how often they should do so, and on relationships between inspecting agencies and those subject to inspection. However, a major underlying theme has been concern that methods of inspection were inappropriate and ineffective. Concentration on regulatory factors such as building standards, staffing arrangements and record keeping, whilst entirely appropriate, has been seen as resulting in the relative exclusion of detailed appraisal of quality of life.

Desire to develop inspection and evaluation methodology so as to focus on quality of life prompted SSI and staff of six social services departments in the North West to set up a project team in April 1988.

Objectives

The main objective of the team was to devise and test a model which would help agencies responsible for providing residential care, and agencies concerned with inspection, to make qualitative evaluations of the performance of residential care homes. Two aspects of 'quality' were identified; one was the care provided by agencies (ie what they did and how they did it), and the other was life as experienced by consumers (ie what it was like to live in a home).

The emphasis of the project was on producing a model for practical application which was based on sound principles and standards, and one which did not have excessive resource implications.

The team's intention was that any model they devised for managers and inspectors as an aid to inspection would also be suitable for use by residential care staff as a focus for self-evaluation and development, and by agencies charged with training those members of staff.

Building the model

The project was tackled in five stages which represented logical progression from principle to practicality as follows:—

1 Principles of residential care were identified by drawing upon the expertise of group members and by referring to publications such as 'A Positive Choice'[1] and 'Home Life'.[2]

References

[1] 'A Positive Choice', Report of an independent review of residential care chaired by Gillian Wagner, OBE, PhD, HMSO London 1988.

[2] 'Home Life': Report of a working party chaired by Kina, Lady Avebury, Centre for Policy on Ageing, London 1984.

2 The many factors which contribute to good quality care and life experience in homes were identified. These were found to group naturally around just six basic values, as follows:—

- PRIVACY
- DIGNITY
- INDEPENDENCE
- CHOICE
- RIGHTS
- FULFILMENT

3 Each value was precisely defined. Statements were made about what a home that was concerned to protect each of these values would be doing. These statements became criteria against which professional judgments could be made about actual standards of practice.

4 For each value, an aide-memoire was designed to translate the statements into discrete areas of investigation, and a framework was devised for collecting and analysing information and comment so as to enable judgments to be made about the extent to which practice matched the criteria.

5 A method of reducing time spent by agencies on regulatory matters was devised as a means of creating space to evaluate quality. This involved asking owners/managers of residential care homes to complete a questionnaire, prior to an inspection. This would provide information that previously would have been collected during the inspection visit, and would offer some indication of whether or not homes were complying with statute, regulation and local authority requirements. Thus the onus was on homes' management to operate their establishments properly, and to provide information in support of this; regulatory authorities would monitor the information and use it as a basis for identifying matters requiring spot checks or investigation during the inspection visit, and would take action regarding information found to be inaccurate.

The result of the work of the group was a series of reference papers or forms, each one containing a full explanation of its intended usage, and each one usable independently or as part of the series, depending on the task in hand. They were designed for use in both statutory and independent sectors as aids for inspection, training and staff development work, and for self monitoring by residential care staff. They were all intended to be shared with all concerned—inspectors, owners and managers of homes, trainers, residential care staff and consumers. Any of them could be used in conjunction with inspection procedures already followed by agencies.

The reference papers and forms have been assembled in this one publication so as to form a comprehensive work of reference and to illustrate how practical tools have been developed from fundamental principles.

The process of building the model

The project team consisted of SSI and local authority members who were assistant directors, homes managers and staff concerned with registration and inspection of independent sector homes. Several team meetings were held over a period of nine months, convened and serviced by SSI; papers prepared by individuals or sub groups were considered at these meetings, and the model was built up in stages.

Between meetings local authority team members involved others in their departments in contributing to the work or acting as sounding boards for the ideas being put forward. Therefore a wide network was created for feeding in ideas and comment, and 'ownership' of the project was extended to a range of SSD staff, including officers in charge and other staff working in residential care homes.

The process of building the model, of thinking through from basic principles to the production of practical tools and involving a wide network of social services department staff, was considered by team members to be of particular value in itself. This has implications in that anyone else proposing to use the model, or any part of it, needs to become immersed in what may be an unfamiliar way of considering issues of quality assurance, and should share it with others, particularly those who might be subjected to inspections based on it. Experience during the pilot studies served to emphasise this.

Testing the model

Seventeen residential care homes were inspected, using all or parts of the model. Of these, thirteen were local authority homes, three were privately owned, and one was run by a voluntary organisation. Inspections were carried out by joint SSI/local authority teams which in some cases included officers in charge.

Two local authorities in particular saw the development and testing of the model as an opportunity to interest a wide variety of staff in considering quality assurance issues and to assess its usefulness as a focus for staff development and training.

Feedback from those using the model for both inspection and staff development purposes, and from those subjected to inspections, led the team to conclude that it should be amended to take account of experience of the pilot studies, and should then be published.

Experience showed that it was a model which could be taken as it was or be adapted to suit particular circumstances. In particular, it was successful in diverting attention away from undue emphasis on buildings, staff numbers, and records in themselves towards assessing such factors in terms of their contribution to quality of life. It helped users to make assessments of quality based on hard evidence, to test the quality of their own practice, and to highlight need for change. It offered a systematic approach to evaluation which would be particularly valuable for less experienced inspectors. In some cases, the process of sharing the model with residents and relatives as a basis for discussing their perspective of the homes, helped to encourage them to comment constructively. Involvement of staff of all kinds enabled them to have a wider and more knowledgeable interest in improving quality in the context of a full appreciation of the standards expected. Furthermore, it helped policy makers and managers to express in more concrete terms what their expectations of homes were.

In terms of content, pilot work showed that initial use of the model was time consuming but far less so than had been anticipated by some participants. Users were confident that it would be manageable as a result of the familiarisation that results from regular usage. There was agreement that principles were sound, and that standards against which practice was measured were what homes should be aspiring to achieve. Although some concepts appeared rather abstract at first, this was overcome because the use of the practical tools enabled users to build up evidence, without overlooking important factors, on which evaluation could be based. There was some repetition when using different forms, but this was beneficial in terms of cross checking evidence. Discussion with staff, and particularly residents and relatives, was facilitated because the model addressed understandable issues using every day language.

Initial apprehension on the part of those inspectors who had not been members of the project team, and those subjected to inspections, was largely allayed by the experience of participation, thus emphasising the value of practical experience. Where those inspected had sight of the model in advance they tended to be less anxious because they knew the standards against which they were to be measured. They had already begun to evaluate their own performance before the inspections, and so a constructive dialogue was possible about policy and practice matters as well as standards in individual homes.

Future developments

Involvement of social services department staff in developing and testing the model has led to their considering how they might use it as part of routine activity.

In terms of inspection work in both local authority and independent sectors, various initiatives are under way. All six social services departments involved in the project are committed to using all or part of the model or to adapting it for specific uses. One is devising a simple means of identifying homes where there appears to be a need to use particular parts of the model in inspection work. Others are adapting it for use in respect of client groups other than elderly people.

Training officers are looking at the potential use of the model in programmes of care assistant training, in particular its relevance to NCVQ developments in terms of measuring and targeting gaps in competencies. It is seen as being particularly useful in this and other aspects of staff development because of its use of every day language and by identifying concrete expressions of abstract concepts. One private home owner proposes to use it as an internal training manual.

The process of building the model had highlighted other related issues requiring attention, but these were not pursued in any detail by the project team; indeed most are issues which each agency may need to consider. Amongst them is the issue of how best to involve residents and relatives and how to structure interviews with them in order to encourage candid and constructive responses. Another is the possibility of grading various aspects of service on a simple scale; this could be a natural extension to the model, but brief discussion by the project team produced very different views about the value of such an approach, and the idea was not fully investigated.

CHAPTER 1

The Principles

Statement of principles of residential care for elderly people upon which the process of inspection and evaluation in Chapters 2, 3 and 4 is based

Introduction

Any model must be rooted in fundamental principles. If an evaluation model is to be accepted as valid by those carrying out evaluations and by those whose activities are under scrutiny, then the principles should be generally understood by people engaged in all aspects of the particular field of interest.

In the field of residential care of elderly people much has been said on this topic in recent years. In drawing up the statement of main principles which underpin good residential care, the authors have drawn on their own experience and on the work of others, notably the bodies chaired by Lady Wagner and Lady Avebury which produced 'A Positive Choice'[1] and 'Home Life'.[2] References indicate where the principles are discussed in those publications.

Principles of residential care for elderly people

1. Residential care should offer old people **the opportunity to enhance their quality of life** by providing a safe, manageable and comfortable environment, plus support and stimulation to help them to maximise their potential physical, intellectual, emotional and social capacity.
   (APC.114, HL.15, HL.45)

2. Residents should be entitled to be **involved in all decisions** affecting their lives unless there are demonstrable reasons why this is not possible or appropriate.
   (APC.35, HL.15, HL.17)

3. The assumption underlying care decisions should be that residents **are capable** of making choices about their own lifestyle (eg holding pension book, medicines, room key, and deciding what to do and when to do it) rather than vice versa unless and until there is clear evidence that the assumption is not valid.
   (APC.36, APC.39, HL.29)

4. Each resident should have a **written contract** agreeing terms and conditions of residence and services to be provided.
   (APC.37)

5. All admissions should be for a **specified trial period** before decisions are made about long term residence.
   (APC.39, HL.18)

6. Homes should offer clear procedures and opportunities for residents to **review** their own situation regularly, along with a friend or adviser and the care managers.
   (APC.34, HL.19)

7. Residents and their representatives should be made aware in writing of a clear **complaints procedure** which includes recourse to persons in authority outwith the home (eg SSD directors or councillors).
   (APC.32, HL.22)

References

[1] 'A Positive Choice', Report of an independent review of residential care chaired by Gillian Wagner, OBE, PhD, HMSO London 1988.

[2] 'Home Life': Report of a working party chaired by Kina, Lady Avebury, Centre for Policy on Ageing, London 1984.

8. All residents retain their **citizen's rights** when they enter residential care, and homes must safeguard these rights and help residents to exercise them.
(APC.114)

9. Homes should seek to ensure that residents continue to have unrestricted access to all **community support services**, including health, social services, leisure and education, and should facilitate such access wherever possible.
(APC.114, HL.23/28)

10. Residents should be able to expect **continuity**, for example in terms of maintaining links with former life (acquaintances, GPs etc), and having personal care provided by a small number of known and trusted staff.

11. Residents are entitled to **'private' accommodation** (ideally single rooms) which they can call their own, which they can use as and when they wish, and to which they can invite guests. This implies choice about the nature of the room or space (eg furnishings) and ability to lock the room and personal belongings.
(HL.23)

12. Homes should ensure that the needs and wishes of all residents are ascertained, respected and met wherever possible, particularly bearing in mind **ethnic, religious and cultural factors**.
(APC.14, HL.16, HL.34)

13. Residents should be able to **retain dignity** and **be treated with dignity**, for example in relation to the manner in which staff handle incontinence problems, bathing or dressing, and the mode of address used to residents.
(HL.15)

14. Staff ethos should be that the **needs of residents are paramount**.
(APC.35, HL.15, HL.17)

15. Homes should guard against restricting rights and choices as a result of **institutional practices** and regimes which emphasise **administrative convenience**.
(APC.15, HL.16, HL.21)

16. Homes should **specify their functions, objectives and services** clearly, and should do so in a way which provides measures against which to assess performance, for instance, in a brochure describing such things as facilities, lifestyle, care philosophy and 'house rules'.
(HL.18)

17. Homes should have procedures for **self monitoring and evaluation** of performance measured against aims and objectives.
(APC.56)

18. Facilities for **day care or other activities not directly related to care** of residents, should be organised and located so as not to interfere with the lifestyle of residents.
(APC.43, HL.18)

19. Residents should be involved in decisions regarding the use of the home for **activities (such as fund raising) which are incompatible** with normal domestic life.
(APC.48)

CHAPTER 2

The reference chart

Chart in matrix form setting out aspects of policy and practice which must be considered when evaluating quality of care and life experience

Introduction

Traditionally, quality of residential care homes has been viewed in terms of a range of categories, such as the suitability of buildings for the consumers concerned, the adequacy of staff numbers or the efficient maintenance of records. Homes have also been assessed to ensure that owners or managers complied with the law and regulations.

However, a model of enquiry based just on these factors is not necessarily enough to enable professional judgements to be made about quality of care given to consumers, or what life in a home actually feels like. It does not necessarily facilitate understanding of the more subtle or intangible aspects of home life.

A way of moving towards doing this is to focus on basic values which underpin quality of life for most people, such as being able to make choices about lifestyle or having human rights safeguarded. It is possible to group the many factors which contribute to quality of life around six such values, as follows:—

PRIVACY —The right of individuals to be left alone or undisturbed and free from intrusion or public attention into their affairs.

DIGNITY —Recognition of the intrinsic value of people regardless of circumstances by respecting their uniqueness and their personal needs; treating with respect.

INDEPENDENCE—Opportunities to act and think without reference to another person, including a willingness to incur a degree of calculated risk.

CHOICE —Opportunity to select independently from a range of options.

RIGHTS —The maintenance of all entitlements associated with citizenship.

FULFILMENT —The realisation of personal aspirations and abilities in all aspects of daily life.

The matrix

The material on the matrix represents all the aspects of policy and practice in residential care which need to be considered in some way when endeavouring to evaluate quality of care provided and quality of life experienced in homes. It is set out in a way which shows the relationship of each aspect to the 'traditional' model on the one hand and to the value based model on the other. The vertical axis of the matrix represents the 'traditional' perspective, expressed in terms of buildings, staff, records etc, whilst the horizontal axis comprises the values of privacy, dignity etc.

The purpose of the matrix is to provide a quick source of reference for anyone concerned with evaluation, whether they be inspectors, managers or owners. It is also suitable for use as a training or staff development aid, for residential care staff who wish to monitor their own practice, or for consumers.

In the aide-memoire and evaluation framework set out in Chapter 4, the material from the matrix has been expanded and translated into specific questions or factors to be observed as part of the evaluation process.

PRIVACY
(The right of individuals to be left alone or undisturbed and free from intrusion or public attention into their affairs).

DIGNITY
(Recognition of the intrinsic value of people regardless of circum by respecting their uniqueness and their personal needs; treatir respect).

PHYSICAL ENVIRONMENT

Privacy
Location of building (eg are bedrooms overlooked? Can residents be overlooked in grounds?)
Personal and private space preferably in private room with door lock.
Personal storage space—lockable—for clothes and valuables.
Privacy in shared rooms—personal and clothes/valuables.
Care in design/layout of sanitary facilities, if not en suite.
Facilities for receiving visitors where residents share bedrooms.
Facilities for reviews and other private discussions.
Variety of types of space in communal areas (alcoves etc).
Suitability of furnishings such as curtains.
Facilities for eating in private.

Dignity
Condition of environment.
Personal space.
Ability to be alone.
Ability to safeguard possessions.
Ability to entertain visitors.
Ability to lock bedroom door.
Access to sanitary facilities if not en suite.
Privacy of sanitary facilities.

CARE PRACTICES

Privacy
'Ownership' of bedroom (knocking on doors etc).
Recognition of residents' needs to be alone at times.
Sensitivity in handling personal matters such as bathing and toileting (eg keeping doors closed).
Sensitivity when discussing personal needs/affairs with residents.
Confidentiality of information about residents (official records or gossip).
Opportunities for residents to discuss problems in private.

Dignity
Mode of address and how determined. 'Patronising' treatment
Knocking on bedroom doors.
Admission process.
Dealing with death.
Sensitivity to needs, feelings and wishes.
Sensitivity in handling bathing, toileting or incontinence.
Sensitivity to cultural and religious needs and special occasions
Respect for idiosyncratic views or behaviour.
Sensitivity in handling medication or financial matters.
Care given to cleanliness and appearance of residents' accomr and clothing.
Are things are done with rather than for residents?
Extent to which practice is geared towards residents' needs rat staff or administrative convenience.
Involvement of relatives or other carers.

STAFF

Privacy
Extent to which selection of staff is on basis of understanding of need to respect privacy.
Adequacy of staff numbers.
Staff attitudes.
Example set by senior staff.
Extent to which rotas (say for cleaning) respect residents' privacy.
Privacy of affairs of staff members (eg nature of sickness if absent).
Support/assistance given to staff by managers.

Dignity
Example set by senior staff. Adequacy of staff numbers.
Is applicants' understanding of dignity a factor in staff selection
Planning of rotas for care rather than administrative convenienc
Do rotas ensure continuity of staff/resident contact?
Amount/nature of resident/staff contact time; 'key worker' or sim systems.
Extent to which staff 'enjoy' being with residents.
Extent to which staff are involved in professional decisions, revie
Stability/consistency of staffing (eg turnover, sickness).
Extent to which staff working environment is conducive to their appropriate care with dignity.
Staff uniforms or other indications of their 'authority' or professic have them, why?

STAFF TRAINING AND DEVELOPMENT

Privacy
Formal qualifications.
Extent to which induction training focuses on privacy
Opportunities for in-service training focusing on privacy.
Staff appraisal/supervision—is account taken of attitude to privacy?
Staff meetings or other arrangements for staff development.
Training of volunteers.
Arrangements to review institutional practices which might unnecessarily intrude on privacy of residents.

Dignity
Formal qualifications.
Extent to which induction training focuses on the skills needed 1 appropriately and sympathetically to needs of residents.
Opportunities for in-service training focusing on maintenance of
Extent to which staff appraisal and supervision arrangements fo dignity of residents. Training of volunteers.
Staff meetings or other means of staff development.
Arrangements to review practices which might infringe dignity.

PROCEDURES

Privacy
Account taken of privacy in procedures such as fire precautions, reviews, complaints, medication, bathing etc.
Arrangements for regular review of procedures to check if appropriate.
Arrangements for residents to gain private access to management.
Reference in staff procedure manual or other documents to privacy.
Arrangements for giving cash or letters to residents.
Involvement of residents in reviews. Access to case records.

Dignity
Arrangements for regular review of procedures.
Do procedures take account of dignity of residents, (eg fire pre access to files, admissions, reviews, complaints, medication)?
Procedures to ensure effective staff communication (eg at shift
Does staff procedure manual or other document emphasise dig
Manner in which letters or cash are given to residents.
Visiting procedures (eg are residents put 'on display'?)

CASE RECORDS

Privacy
Confidentiality of information (how and where kept).
Condition of case files.
Accessibility of case records (who, when, why?)
Departmental policy and practice relating to residents' access to records.

Dignity
Confidentiality of information about residents.
Access to residents' files (policy and practice).
Extent to which residents' files contain information which helps provide care in a manner which is sensitive to residents' back problems, preferences etc (eg personal, medical).
How records are used, and why (eg bath books, residents' sav clothing books).

DOCUMENTS

Privacy
Reference to privacy in brochure or other publicity material.
Reference to privacy in contracts.
Indications in daily diary or other records about extent to which privacy is respected.

Dignity
Does brochure indicate concern for maintaining dignity?
Existence or otherwise of contracts which specify what residents for their money. Do they know where they stand?
Indications in daily diary or other records about extent to which respected.

MEALS AND MEALTIMES

Privacy
Flexibility in providing for the needs of people who may wish to eat in private (eg people with socially unacceptable habits).

Dignity
Are residents' wishes ascertained and respected?
Manner in which staff handle situations where residents may off by their table behaviour.
Provision made for residents who wish to eat alone because of table behaviour caused by illness or disability.
Procedure at table (eg do residents serve themselves and othe
Arrangements for residents to entertain visitors to meals.

CHAPTER 3

Pre-inspection Questionnaire

Form to be sent to owners or managers of residential care homes requesting information prior to inspection visits

The model for evaluating quality of care provided and life experienced in residential care homes has a number of potential users, such as inspectors, managers, owners, care staff, trainers and perhaps consumers. When used for inspections there is an additional dimension to the process which arises by virtue of the fact that inspectors come from outwith the homes and so have a need to build up information bases as the first steps in carrying out evaluations. Factual information is also required so as to establish whether or not homes are complying with statute, regulations and local authority standards.

Much of this information does not necessarily have to be obtained during inspection visits but can be collected beforehand as an administrative process. This questionnaire is proposed as the means of so doing.

As well as providing the inspecting agency with essential information about buildings, staff, record keeping etc, completion of the questionnaire prior to inspections will have a significant impact on the efficiency of the inspection process. It will:—

● drastically reduce the amount of owners', managers', and inspectors' time spent on basic information collection during inspection visits, thus freeing time for inspectors to concentrate on quality of life and care provided;

● provide inspectors with information which may help them to identify areas of enquiry on which to concentrate during inspection visits;

● give owners or managers responsibility for stating that they are complying with regulations and local authority requirements, and providing the service described in their brochures or other documents, thus freeing inspectors to make spot checks rather than full investigations on every visit; and

● give owners or managers opportunity to draw inspectors' attention to any issues which need to be discussed during inspection visits.

Notes for respondents (owners or managers)

Owners or managers of homes should complete the questionnaire, sign and date the panel on this page, and submit it to the inspecting agency one week before the on-site inspection.

If some of the information requested on the questionnaire is already given fully in homes' brochures, plans or other documents already in the possession of the inspecting agency, it would be appropriate for the owners or managers to refer inspectors to this rather than repeat the information in full.

On the second and subsequent occasions that the questionnaire is used for a particular home, it would be appropriate for the owner or manager merely to indicate changes or 'no change from last inspection' where appropriate rather than complete full details every time.

The final question of each section is added merely to give respondents an opportunity to raise issues which they feel need to be discussed with the inspecting agency. A 'nil' response would be quite appropriate if there were no such issues.

Name and designation
of person completing
form

_____

Date completed

Name and address of home to be inspected
Date of visit
Name of inspector(s)
Name of inspecting agency

Notes for inspecting agency

The questionnaire is designed to be adaptable for use in respect of any residential care home for elderly people in both local authority and independent sectors. It is designed to elicit basic factual information only, and is not intended to present a comprehensive picture of each home and life within it.

Before sending the blank questionnaire to the owner or manager, the inspecting agency should complete the panel on this page, and ensure that questions which do not apply to the home in question are deleted.

The questionnaire should be sent to the owner or manager early enough to allow him/her adequate time (at least two weeks) to complete and return it by about a week before the inspection visit. This should allow time for inspectors to study the contents in order to identify matters requiring further investigation during the inspection visit, and, where appropriate, to transfer information to the framework for evaluating quality which is set out in Chapter 4.

1. BASIC INFORMATION

1.1 Name and address of owner.

1.2 Name and address of manager.

1.3 Categories of registration.

1.4 What other facilities not directly concerned with residents (eg day care, sheltered housing, social services offices) are there?

1.5 Is the house divided into group units, say, for semi-independence?

YES/NO

1.6 Is there a brochure?

YES/NO

If YES, please send a copy with this form, and say if it is available in languages other than English.

If NO, please send any already prepared statement of philosophy, aims and objectives.

1.7 Where home is owned by a local authority, private company/individual or voluntary agency, based elsewhere, please state how often the establishment has been inspected by them during the past year.

1.8 Are copies of reports of such inspections available at the home for scrutiny by inspectors?

YES/NO

If NO, where are they kept?

1.9 Does the population of the home's catchment area comprise a significant proportion of people from minority ethnic groups?

YES/NO

If YES, give brief details.

2. RESIDENTS

2.1 Number of places—long stay. ☐

short stay. ☐

2.2 Number of residents on date of completing this form. ☐

Is this a typical level of occupancy? **YES/NO**

2.3 Number of admissions in past year. ☐

Number of discharges in past year. ☐

Number of deaths in the home in past year. ☐

(If a substantial number of admissions were short stay placements, please say so).

2.4 In what circumstances, and for how long, are beds retained for absent residents?

2.5 If there are any residents from minority ethnic groups, please give brief details of their numbers and groups.

2.6 Has there been a recent analysis of residents, in terms of physical and mental condition, using a validated dependency rating scale? (eg Crighton Royal) **YES/NO**

If YES, please submit a copy of the findings.

2.7 Number of residents on the date of completing this form who were:

● bedfast ☐

● mentally confused ☐

● regularly incontinent of urine ☐

● regularly doubly incontinent ☐

● chairbound ☐

● exhibiting extreme behaviour ☐

2.8 Number of residents on the date of completing this form requiring:

- dressing

- feeding

- washing

- bathing

- toileting

2.9 Are case files kept for all residents?

YES/NO

2.10 Are there policies/procedures regarding access by residents to their personal records?

YES/NO

If YES, please submit a copy and say if it is available in languages other than English.

2.11 Do residents each have a written contract with the management specifying terms and conditions of residence and services/facilities to be provided?

YES/NO

If YES, please submit a blank copy, and say if it is available in languages other than English.

2.12 Do residents have a copy of a written complaints procedure?

YES/NO

If YES, please submit a copy, and say if it is available in languages other than English.

2.13 Is a record kept of all complaints made, and the results of the investigations.

YES/NO

2.14 How many complaints have there been during the past year?

2.15 Please list any general issues regarding residents which you would like to discuss with the inspection officer.

3.   FINANCE

3.1 What is the current scale of charges to residents per week? Please explain if it is a fixed scale or whether charges differ according to quality of accommodation or services given.

3.2 What additional charges are levied, and what for?

3.3 Do all residents receive a personal allowance to spend on themselves as they wish?   **YES/NO**

3.4 Do you keep records of the management of personal allowances?   **YES/NO**

3.5 How many clients resident on the date of completing this form kept their own pension book? How many handled all their own financial affairs?

3.6 In how many cases on the date of completing this form was the owner/manager the nominee for handling residents' financial affairs?

3.7 Where are savings invested for residents who do not handle their own affairs (eg bank, local authority account, building society)?

3.8 Give the date of the last visit by auditors to review the home's financial conduct.

3.9 Please list any financial matters which you would like to discuss with the inspecting officer.

4. PREMISES

4.1 Please submit a scale plan of the home, indicating use of all rooms, including single/multiple usage, semi-independence groups or other special facilities. (If plans have already been submitted please indicate any changes of structure or usage since the last inspection together with date of local authority approval in the case of independent homes).

4.2 What facilities are there for routine servicing and emergency repair work to lifts/stairlifts?

4.3 What facilities are there for residents to receive visitors?

4.4 Give the dates of the most recent inspection visits by:

- fire prevention officer

- environmental health officer

- gas/electricity boards

- fire equipment manufacturers (appliances, alarm systems etc)

4.5 Has all the work recommended by these bodies been done?

YES/NO

If NO, what plans are in hand to complete the work?

4.6 How many fire drills have been held in the past year and what was the date of the last one?

4.7 Please list any matters regarding premises which you wish to discuss with the inspecting officer.

5. HEALTH/SOCIAL CARE

5.1 Does the home have a written policy and procedures for assessing and reviewing the condition of residents and their needs?

YES/NO

If YES, please submit a copy.

5.2 What arrangements are made for the provision of personal clothing (eg visit to home by supplier, visit to shop, bulk buying) and how is payment made (cash, cheque, order book etc)?

5.3 What rules/procedures (if any) are there for visiting?

5.4 What arrangements are made to help residents to continue religious observance if desired, and to follow customs/practices related to their racial/cultural background?

5.5 What arrangements are there for regular checks on residents' general health, hearing, eyesight, teeth and feet?

5.6 How many residents keep and administer their own medication?

5.7 Name the members of staff (and their job titles) who are responsible for the safekeeping, handling and disposal of drugs.

5.8 Are there written policies/ procedures relating to the handling of drugs?

YES/NO

If YES, please submit a copy.

5.9 Please list any issues relating to health and social care which you would like to discuss with the inspecting officer.

6. STAFFING

6.1 In order to give an overview of staffing structure and composition, please give information about staff members.

Name (indicate if male/female)	Designation	Formal qualifications in residential and related work including catering	Tick age group			
			−20	21/30	31/50	51+

6.2 How many staff are there at night?

  ● On 'waking' duty.

  ● Sleeping on premises 'on call'.

  ● Available elsewhere if required in an emergency.

6.3 What are the arrangements for staff cover in the absence of the owner or manager?

6.4 Please submit a copy of a full cycle of duty rotas.

6.5 Do staff have written job descriptions?

YES/NO

If YES, please submit a sample of each (eg manager, care assistant, domestic worker etc).

6.6 In the past year how many staff have:

  ● commenced employment

  ● ceased employment

6.7 Are there any policy/ procedure/statements about recruitment, staff meetings, use training and support of volunteers, staff complaints/ disciplinary procedures, health and safety at work, induction and other training, supervision and activities of students?

YES/NO

If YES, please submit copies.

6.8 Please list any staffing issues which you would like to discuss with the inspecting officer.

7. MEALS AND MEALTIMES

7.1 List times of main meals:

- breakfast

- lunch

- evening meal

- supper

(If there are no fixed times, please say so.)

7.2 Is a record kept of menus or meals served? **YES/NO**

If YES, please submit a copy of the record for the last month.

7.3 Do residents have a choice of menus? **YES/NO**

7.4 Are the dietary needs and wishes of people from minority ethnic groups met? **YES/NO**

7.5 Are special diets provided for medical reasons? **YES/NO**

7.6 Are there any facilities for residents or their visitors to prepare drinks or snacks? **YES/NO**

7.7 Please list any matters regarding meals/mealtimes which you would like to discuss with the inspecting officer.

8. RECORDS

8.1 Do you keep the undermentioned records?

- Daily register of residents. **YES/NO**

- Case records for every resident. **YES/NO**

- Daily occurrence and staff handover book (or diary). **YES/NO**

- Record of medicines kept in the home, who they are prescribed for, when dispensed, any destroyed or returned to pharmacy, and balance of all medicines held at any time. **YES/NO**

- Menus, diet sheets or record of meals served. **YES/NO**

- Record of fire drills and equipment testing. **YES/NO**

- Record for each resident showing money or other valuables received on their behalf and how it has been disposed of by the registered person. **YES/NO**

- Records for each employee in the home (with references, contract of employment, pay levels etc). **YES/NO**

- Record of accidents to staff or residents in the home. **YES/NO**

8.2 Please list any aspects of record keeping which you would like to discuss with the inspecting officer.

CHAPTER 4

The aide-memoire and evaluation framework

Checklist and recording format for each of the following:—

- Privacy
- Dignity
- Independence
- Choice
- Rights
- Fulfilment

Introduction

This chapter takes forward the notion of evaluating quality of care provided and quality of life experienced in homes, in relation to basic values. It introduces a series of six forms, each of which deals with one of the following:—

PRIVACY —The right of individuals to be left alone or undisturbed and free from intrusion or public attention into their affairs

DIGNITY —Recognition of the intrinsic value of people regardless of circumstances by respecting their uniqueness and their personal needs; treating with respect

INDEPENDENCE—Opportunities to act and think without reference to another person, including a willingness to incur a degree of calculated risk

CHOICE —Opportunity to select independently from a range of options

RIGHTS —The maintenance of all entitlements associated with citizenship

FULFILMENT —The realisation of personal aspirations and abilities in all aspects of daily life

Each form contains an aide-memoire, a framework for gathering and analysing information, and clear criteria against which judgements can be made about quality of practice.

Whilst the forms are designed primarily for inspection work, they are equally suitable for self-monitoring by residential care managers and staff, and as aids for staff training and development.

Each form can be used separately as a specific focus of investigation. Each one can be used in tandem with others so as to achieve a wider view of a home. Each one can be used as one component of a comprehensive evaluation. When used for inspection work the forms should be used in conjunction with the pre-inspection questionnaire so that essential background information is to hand.

Notes for users

In each form the first column on the left hand side lists the recommended areas of investigation and specific topics to be addressed by the inspector (not necessarily questions to be posed to those being inspected). The other three columns provide for recording responses to such investigations obtained from three sources, namely written material, discussion and observation. Each framework is designed to assist inspectors to assimilate the information from these sources and make comparisons where appropriate, for instance between stated policy and observed practice. At the bottom of each page is a space for recording other comments or 'feelings' about life in homes. Whether or not the forms are carried around homes and completed on the spot, or used simply as 'prompts' is up to the persons using them, as long as at some point in time all information is recorded in the framework.

On each form there is space for recording a concise evaluation, based on an overview of the responses in the framework. Evaluations should relate findings to the criteria of a 'good' home outlined under 'Suggested criteria for evaluation' and should identify areas of good or questionable practice. Evaluations should concentrate particularly upon areas that should be improved and should offer constructive advice as to how improvements might be achieved.

Each inspecting agency will have its own procedures for reporting back to owners/managers following inspections, both orally at the homes at the conclusion of visits, and later in writing. The contents of evaluation frameworks, when completed, could be shared with those subjected to inspections or could simply form the basis of separate reports. A suggested model for a written report is shown in Chapter 5.

Privacy

The aide-memoire and evaluation framework

Name and address of home inspected
Date of visit
Name of inspector(s)
Name of inspecting agency

Suggested criteria for Evaluation

The focus of this particular framework is PRIVACY, which is defined as '*The right of individuals to be left alone or undisturbed and free from intrusion or public attention into their affairs*'.

The suggested 'yardstick' against which performance (as indicated by the comment and information in the framework) should be measured, is a notion of what a home which actively seeks to safeguard and enhance various aspects of privacy would be like. Such a 'good' home will seek to:—

1   have some knowledge of residents' previous lifestyles so as to understand their expectations regarding personal privacy;

2   identify residents' preferences regarding the extent to which they wish to associate with other residents, and in what circumstances;

3   ensure that residents can meet people, have conversations, make or receive telephone calls, correspond and receive visitors, without being overlooked or overheard and without having to account to anyone for their actions;

4   ensure that residents can bathe, wash and use the toilet without being overlooked or overheard, and that they are protected from intrusion whether accidental, deliberate or routine;

5   ensure that where staff assistance is required to enable residents to dress, bathe, wash or use the toilet, this is kept to the minimum commensurate with residents' abilities and is performed with due regard to the need to safeguard the privacy of the individual;

6   make suitable arrangements for residents to discuss personal matters with staff and visitors in private;

7   ensure that staff deal discreetly with the affairs of residents and safeguard the confidentiality of information held about them;

8   ensure that essential housekeeping and administrative procedures intrude as little as possible on the privacy of individuals or groups;

9   create safeguards to ensure that any erosion of privacy that is considered by 'management' to be necessary in order to provide essential care for individuals, is explained, justified and reviewed regularly; and

10   create a physical environment which protects people from public gaze, which allows choice of whether to be alone or in company, which provides personal and private spaces for every individual, which provides for security of information and personal possessions, and in which shared facilities such as bathrooms and toilets are designed to ensure that personal activities can be conducted in complete privacy.

Evaluation

NOTE FOR USERS. When you have pursued your investigations into the home, using the aide memoire contained in the following pages, the findings you have recorded on the framework should be drawn on to produce an overall evaluation. Brief comments expressed in one or two sentences should be made in respect of each of the elements of a 'good' home outlined under 'Suggested criteria for evaluation' and there should be a general conclusion.

General conclusions

The right of individuals to be left alone or undisturbed and free from intrusion or public attention into their affairs

Aide Memoire

Extent to which acceptance of people's needs and rights for privacy and confidentiality is a part of the *home's ethos*

Written Information

Information available from pre inspection questionnaire, plans, brochures and other documents seen before or during the inspection

Does owner/agency recognise people's right and need for personal privacy and confidentiality of information
● in brochure or other publicity?
● in day to day management?

Do staff *understand* the importance of personal privacy and confidentiality of information?
● Is it covered in induction training?
● Is it part of other training?
● Is it mentioned in any records of training events?
● Is it discussed at recruitment interviews?
● Is it discussed at staff meetings?
● Is it mentioned in the staff meeting minutes?
● Is it referred to in the staff manual?
● Have staff undertaken formal training (eg CSS)?
● Do staff have any performance appraisal?

Do *residents and relatives* appear to understand their rights to privacy and confidentiality?
● Is there a fact sheet for potential and new residents?
● Do contracts mention privacy/confidentiality?
● What are people told before admission?

Do *volunteers* or people on *special schemes* (eg ET) understand importance of privacy and confidentiality?
● Do they have any training?
● Do they have specific tasks/contracts?

General comment on matters not covered by these questions, and reactions/feelings of inspectors which do not fit into the response column above

Discussion

Information and comment from discussion with owner/manager, staff, residents and other people such as relatives and friends

Observation

Observations of inspector regarding attitudes, care practices, facilities, procedures, activities etc seen or heard during inspection

FORM **A** PRIVACY

(The right of individuals to be left alone or undisturbed and free from intrusion or public attention into their affairs)

Aide Memoire

Extent to which *care practice* recognises and caters for residents' rights and needs for personal privacy and confidentiality of information

Do staff *respect* privacy of bedrooms?
- Do they knock on doors?
- Do they wait to be invited in?
- Are official and other visitors shown bedrooms without occupant's permission?

What arrangements are there to *explain and review* situations where privacy is infringed for good care reasons?

Are residents able to be *alone* in their bedrooms when they wish? Can they entertain guests in their rooms?

Are residents able to be *alone* in other parts of the building or grounds?

How do staff handle *official or other visitors*?
- Are they introduced to residents when being shown around?
- Is residents' permission sought?
- Do staff explain to residents who visitors are and why they are there?

How do staff ensure appropriate privacy when *bathing or toileting* residents?
- Are doors properly closed?
- Where do residents undress?
- If there is a toileting regime for certain residents, are steps taken to make it less obvious to others?

Is privacy infringed by *routines*?
- Is bedroom cleaning arranged to fit clients' routines, or vice versa?
- Do staff numbers and rotas allow for flexibility of routines?
- Are bedrooms doors kept ajar at night so staff can observe residents?
- Does night supervision include routine entering of bedrooms?

General comment on matters not covered by these questions, and reactions/feelings of inspector which do not fit into the response columns above

Written Information

Information available from pre inspection questionnaire, plans, brochures and other documents seen before or during the inspection

Discussion
Information and comment from discussion with owner/manager, staff, residents and other people such as relatives and friends

Observation
Observations of inspector regarding attitudes, care practices, facilities, procedures, activities etc seen or heard during inspection

Aide Memoire

Extent to which *care practice* recognises and caters for residents' rights and needs for personal privacy and confidentiality of information (continued)

Written Information

Information available from pre inspection questionnaire, plans, brochures and other documents seen before or during the inspection

Are there *routines* to improve privacy, (eg closing toilet doors when clients fail to do so?) Are routines regularly reviewed?

What arrangements are there for people who wish, or need, to *eat* in private.
● by choice?
● because of socially unacceptable behaviour of self or others?

Staff privacy
● Do staff have access to manager to discuss personal matters?
● Are staff ever reprimanded publicly?
● Are staff matters discussed in front of residents?
● If staff receive supervision, is it conducted in private?

Do residents have access to managers to discuss *personal affairs* in private?
● At any time?
● Where? (office/bedroom/elsewhere)
● If in office, do staff close door?

What is procedure for giving *cash or mail* to residents?
● Letter box in bedroom?
● Handed over in bedroom?
● Handed over in lounge or at table?
● Collected from office or notice board?

Confidentiality of *information*
● Are case files locked away?
● What information is shared with staff (eg key workers) and how is this done?
● Do staff ensure that staff discussion about residents is done privately? (eg do they close office door?)
● Do staff gossip about residents?

General comment on matters not covered by these questions, and reactions/feelings of inspector which do not fit into the response columns above

Discussion

Information and comment from discussion with owner/manager, staff, residents and other people such as relatives and friends

Observation

Observations of inspector regarding attitudes, care practices, facilities, procedures, activities etc seen or heard during inspection

Aide Memoire

Extent to which *buildings and grounds* provide for privacy of residents, their belongings and affairs

Written Information

Information available from pre inspection questionnaire, plans, brochures and other documents seen before or during the inspection

---

Is the *location* of the home appropriate?
- Are bedrooms overlooked?
- Are public rooms open to view of passers-by?
- Can residents be overlooked in the grounds?
- Would unconventional behaviour (eg wandering) be easily noticeable to passers-by?
- Is it in an area subject to excessive noise, vandalism, trespass etc?

Does the home provide appropriate *security*? (eg window or door design, alarm systems etc)

How many people have *single* bedrooms?
- Can bedroom doors be locked?
- Can people see into the rooms when doors are closed (eg spy holes, internal windows)

How many bedrooms house 2, 3, 4 or more residents?
- Do occupants have identified personal space?
- Are there screens?
- Is furniture arranged to enhance privacy?
- Can residents use wash basins in private?

Do bedrooms have appropriate *storage space* for clothes and personal possessions?
- Does each occupant have his/her own furniture?
- Are cupboards and drawers lockable?
- Can people with physical handicap reach cupboards or turn keys and handles?

Do bedrooms have appropriate curtains or blinds?

General comment on matters not covered by these questions, and reactions/feelings of inspector which do not fit into the response columns above

Discussion

Information and comment from discussion with owner/manager, staff, residents and other people such as relatives and friends

Observation

Observations of inspector regarding attitudes, care practices, facilities, procedures, activities etc seen or heard during inspection

(The right of individuals to be left alone or undisturbed and free from intrusion or public attention into their affairs)

Aide Memoire

Extent to which *buildings and grounds* provide for privacy of residents, their belongings and affairs (continued)

Written Information

Information available from pre inspection questionnaire, plans, brochures and other documents seen before or during the inspection

---

Are shared bathrooms and toilets suitably located, designed and equipped?
- Can doors be locked (with provision for emergency entry)?
- Is there adequate space in toilets and bathrooms to enable easy closing of doors by people with physical handicaps, (frames, wheelchairs etc)
- Are rooms equipped with aids for handicapped people so they can cope alone if desired? (bath seats, grip rails, alarm system etc)

Are there private facilities for residents in shared bedrooms to receive visitors?

Does the building allow privacy for individuals or small groups (other than bedrooms), say, in small sitting rooms, alcoves etc?
Can phone calls be made in private?

Do dining facilities allow for residents with handicaps or illnesses which cause unsocial eating habits to eat separately, in part of dining room or elsewhere?

Are there private facilities for reviews and other discussions, say, in
- conference/interview room?
- office?
- staff room?

Are there proper facilities to store and safeguard confidential papers, case files etc?

General comment on matters not covered by these questions, and reactions/feelings of inspector which do not fit into the response columns above

Discussion

Information and comment from discussion with owner/manager, staff, residents and other people such as relatives and friends

Observation

Observations of inspector regarding attitudes, care practices, facilities, procedures, activities etc seen or heard during inspection

Dignity

The aide-memoire and evaluation framework

Name and address of
home inspected

_____

Date of visit

_____

Name of inspector(s)

_____

Name of inspecting agency

Suggested criteria for evaluation

The focus of this particular framework is DIGNITY, which is defined as *'A recognition of the intrinsic value of people regardless of cir-cumstances by respecting their uniqueness and their personal needs; treating with respect'.*

The suggested 'yardstick' against which performance (as indicated by the comment and information in the framework) should be measured, is a notion of what a home which actively helps people living there to lead dignified lives would be like. Such a 'good' home will seek to:—

1   establish a clear philosophy of care based on a recognition of the worth of all residents and their right to be treated with respect and to be helped to live in a dignified manner;

2   put the wishes of residents, and their relatives and advisers where appropriate, at the centre of decision making regarding their own care and treatment; make decisions with rather than for residents and take note of and act in response to complaints;

3   have knowledge and understanding of the whole person in terms of his or her current situation and past life experience, taking account of cultural, religious and other needs and norms;

4   ensure that when, because of infirmity, residents require assistance with personal aspects of care this is done sensitively and in private by persons who are known, trusted and (where possible) chosen by residents;

5   safeguard by sensitive and attentive care the dignity of residents who, because of absent mindedness or infirmity, are not always in control of their behaviour or their appearance in terms of cleanli-ness, condition of clothing or offensiveness to others;

6   help residents to have a sense of ownership of personal living space and acceptance of shared responsibility for the wider home environment;

7   ensure that residents know what information is kept about them and how it is used, and that they have confidence that its confidentiality will be respected; and

8   provide an appropriately designed and equipped environment in which residents can look after their own personal care to the fullest extent commensurate with their level of infirmity.

Evaluation

NOTE FOR USERS When you have pursued your investigations into the home, using the aide memoire contained in the following pages, the findings you have recorded on the framework should be drawn on to produce an overall evaluation. Brief comments expressed in one or two sentences should be made in respect of each of the elements of a 'good' home outlined under 'Suggested criteria for evaluation', and there should be a general conclusion.

General conclusions

(A recognition of the intrinsic value of people regardless of circumstances respecting their uniqueness and their personal needs; treating with respec

Aide memoire

Care philosophy of home and how it is communicated

Written information

Information available from pre inspection questionnaire, plans, brochures and other documents seen before or during the inspection

Does the owner/manager *promote* maintenance of dignity as a major objective, say,
- in brochure or publicity material?
- in day to day management?

Is there a *philosophy* statement?
- Where is it kept?
- Who sees it?
- Who contributes to it?
- When and how is it received?
- Is it really implemented?

Does philosophy statement include things like:
- treating residents as adults?
- respecting residents as 'elders'?
- avoiding patronising treatment?
- not putting people 'on display' to visitors?
- involvement in decision making?

Do *clients and relatives* understand that admission to a home should not mean loss of dignity?
- What written material is supplied before and on arrival?
- Does material give accurate picture?

Do staff arrangements *reflect* philosophy?
- Numbers of contacts, key workers etc
- Balance of part/full time staff
- How are staff made aware of importance of dignity (eg induction, ongoing training, senior staff example, home's ethos etc)?
- Do job descriptions refer to dignity?

General comment on matters not covered by these questions, and reactions/feelings of inspector which do not fit into the response columns above

Discussion

Information and comment from discussion with owner/manager, staff, residents and other people such as relatives and friends

Observation

Observations of inspector regarding attitudes, care practices, facilities, procedures, activities etc seen or heard during inspection

(A recognition of the intrinsic value of people regardless of circumstances by respecting their uniqueness and their personal needs; treating with respect.)

Aide memoire
Treatment of people as individuals, involvement of residents in decision making, recognising cultural needs and norms

Written information
Information available from pre inspection questionnaire, plans, brochures and other documents seen before or during the inspection

Extent to which *people are involved* with making decisions about themselves.
- Is there an admission procedure?
- Are there pre-admission visits?
- Are relatives involved in admissions?
- Are people encouraged to manage their affairs (eg finance, medicines)?

Are people treated as *individuals*?
- Do staff get to know people?
- Do staff know about people's backgrounds and life experiences?
- Are there key workers?
- Are staff numbers adequate?
- How are people encouraged to retain and share life experiences?
- Can people individualise bedrooms?
- Is clothing personal to each client?
- Are residents ever 'pressurised' to join functions or outings?

Recognition of *cultural needs and norms*
- What modes of address are used?
- Who decides on mode of address?
- Is there an appropriate staff mix—gender, race, culture?
- Do staff know about minority cultures?
- Is there choice of menus, and how are residents informed?
- How is death handled (individually/collectively, open/secret)?
- Can people choose who bathes them?
- Are there rules about smoking and alcohol which take account of dignity of consumers and others?

How are *complaints* handled?
- Do residents know procedure?
- Are complaints treated seriously?
- Is procedure effective and appropriate?

General comment on matters not covered by these questions, and reactions/feelings of inspector which do not fit into the response columns above

Discussion

Information and comment from discussion with owner/manager, staff, residents and other people such as relatives and friends

Observation

Observations of inspector regarding attitudes, care practices, facilities, procedures, activities etc seen or heard during inspection

Aide memoire
Care practices in relation to living patterns and situations arising from infirmity of residents

Written information
Information available from pre inspection questionnaire, plans, brochures and other documents seen before or during the inspection

Do care practices focus on clients' *living* patterns or staff *convenience*?
● How flexible are mealtimes?
● Can people choose when to rise/retire/bathe?
● Are there set visiting hours?
● Is the medicine routine a 'personalised' or 'medical' model?
● How are staff rotas arranged?
● Can people decide how they arrange and in what condition they keep bedrooms?

Do care practices relate to *individuals*?
● Continuity of staff/resident relationships?
● Key worker or similar system?
● Is there a high staff turnover?
● Are residents 'patronised' when confused or lost?
● Is incontinence handled sensitively, is there a sensitive 'toileting' procedure where necessary?
● Do staff keep an eye on residents' appearance (general appropriateness of clothes, cleanliness, dressing properly after using toilet etc)?
● How do staff deal with situations where residents may behave unconventionally at dining table, because of infirmity?
● Are residents allowed time to do things?

How is a *sense of 'home'* created?
● Can people bring with them furniture and personal effects?
● Can people choose furniture/decor?
● Can people be alone?
● Can relatives/friends stay overnight?
● Can people 'personalise' their own spaces in shared bedrooms?
● Can residents share in decisions about other parts of the home (eg house meetings, suggestion box)?

General comment on matters not covered by these questions, and reactions/feelings of inspector which do not fit into the response columns above

Discussion
Information and comment from discussion with owner/manager, staff, residents and other people such as relatives and friends

Observation
Observations of inspector regarding attitudes, care practices, facilities, procedures, activities etc seen or heard during inspection

Aide memoire
Confidentiality of information

Written information
Information available from pre inspection questionnaire, plans, brochures and other documents seen before or during the inspection

Ownership/maintenance of *personal* files:—
- How is personal information recorded about clients and staff?
- Where is personal information kept?
- What guidelines does the agency give about recording content/method?
- What procedures exist for monitoring/reviewing content of records?
- Who contributes/writes records?
- Do people know what is written about them?
- Do people see records?
- What is access procedure?
- Do people contribute to own file? Are they encouraged to do so (care plans, reviews, contracts)?

Security of *personal* information:—
- Where are files kept?
- Are they locked away securely?
- Is the room door always locked when not occupied?
- Who has keys to the filing cabinet and the room?

Staff practices:—
- What information about residents is made available to staff at various levels? Is this official policy?
- Is personal information discussed at staff meetings?
- Do staff gossip about residents?
- Is there a reasonable balance between sharing information about residents which contributes to care decisions, and confidentiality?

General comment on matters not covered by these questions, and reactions/feelings of inspector which do not fit into the response columns above

Discussion

Information and comment from discussion with owner/manager, staff, residents and other people such as relatives and friends

Observation

Observations of inspector regarding attitudes, care practices, facilities, procedures, activities etc seen or heard during inspection

(A recognition of the intrinsic value of people regardless of circumstances by respecting their uniqueness and their personal needs; treating with respect.)

Aide memoire
Buildings and equipment

Written information
Information available from pre inspection questionnaire, plans, brochures and other documents seen before or during the inspection

How is the building's *design and structure* used to enhance people's abilities?
- Are there areas restricted to staff or visitors?
- How is furniture arranged?
- Is there choice of communal living rooms?
- Can large living rooms be sub-divided?
- Are there adequate bathrooms/wc's?
- Is there an appropriate range of bath/wc types?
- Are baths/wc's convenient for bedrooms?
- Are there garden/outside facilities?
- Is exterior accessible?

Does building *help safeguard* dignity?
- Are there locks on doors to bedrooms, bathrooms, wcs? Are locks of appropriate design? Do they work?
- Do people have single rooms?
- Can residents lock away possessions in private or shared rooms?
- Are there facilities for people to see visitors, health professionals etc in privacy?
- Are there mirrors in bedroom, bathroom, wc, so residents can check their appearance?

Suitability of equipment so infirm people can help themselves as much as possible:—
- Are there aids for dressing?
- Are sink tap handles appropriate?
- Can people reach cupboards?
- Are there adequate bath rails?
- Are baths non-slip?
- Is cutlery and crockery designed for infirm people available where appropriate?

General comment on matters not covered by these questions, and reactions/feelings of inspector which do not fit into the response columns above

Discussion
Information and comment from discussion with owner/manager, staff, residents and other people such as relatives and friends

Observation
Observations of inspector regarding attitudes, care practices, facilities, procedures, activities etc seen or heard during inspection

Independence

The aide-memoire and evaluation framework

Name and address of home inspected
Date of visit
Name of inspector(s)
Name of inspecting agency

Suggested criteria for evaluation

The focus of this particular framework is INDEPENDENCE, which is defined as *'Opportunities to think and act without reference to another person including a willingness to incur a degree of calculated risk'*.

The suggested 'yardstick' against which performance (as indicated by the comment and information in the framework) should be measured, is a notion of what a home which actively helps residents to achieve a level of independence compatible with their wishes and abilities will be like. Such a 'good' home will seek to:—

1   have some knowledge of residents' previous lifestyles and consult with them and their relatives/advisers so as to understand their expectations and wishes regarding independence;

2   help and encourage residents to think and act independently as far as this is compatible with their own abilities, their impact on other people, the constraints of communal life, and the risks involved;

3   encourage and enable residents to participate in making decisions about home life in general insofar as they wish and are able to do so;

4   ascertain the views of residents about any proposed action which would affect their lifestyle in the home;

5   provide a physical environment which enables residents to do as much as possible for themselves without having to rely on staff assistance or having things done for them;

6   monitor each resident's condition and behaviour so as to ensure that a reasonable balance is achieved between independence and risk taking; and

7   create safeguards to ensure that any limitations placed on residents' scope to act independently are explained, justified and reviewed regularly.

Evaluation

NOTE FOR USERS When you have pursued your investigations into the home, using the aide memoire contained in the following pages, the findings you have recorded on the framework should be drawn on to produce an overall evaluation. Brief comments expressed in one or two sentences should be made in respect of each of the elements of a 'good' home outlined under 'Suggested criteria for evaluation', and there should be a general conclusion.

General conclusions

(Opportunities to think and act without reference to another person including a willingness to incur a degree of calculated risk.)

Aide memoire
Extent to which residents' rights to think and act independently forms part of the *home's ethos*

Written information
Information available from pre inspection questionnaire, plans, brochures and other documents seen before or during the inspection

Does *owner/agency* recognise the value of retaining independence in
- brochure or other publicity?
- contracts with residents?

If there is a *policy* statement
- What is the policy?
- What does it say about risk taking?
- Who knows about it?

Do *staff and volunteers* understand that residents should be as independent as possible?
- Have they a copy of the policy statement?
- Is it covered in induction training?
- Is it part of other training?
- Is it mentioned in records of training events?
- Is it discussed at recruitment interviews?
- Is it discussed at staff meetings? Is it in the minutes?
- Is it in job descriptions?
- Is it referred to in staff manual?
- Is it mentioned in daily records?
- Is it covered in staff supervision?
- Have staff had formal training (eg CSS) which might help appreciate the importance of encouraging independence?

Do *residents and relatives/advisers* understand about independence? Is it mentioned in any contracts, brochure, or fact sheet for potential and new residents?

General comment on matters not covered by these questions, and reactions/feelings of inspector which do not fit into the response columns above

Discussion

Information and comment from discussion with owner/manager, staff, residents and other people such as relatives and friends

Observation

Observations of inspector regarding attitudes, care practices, facilities, procedures, activities etc seen or heard during inspection

Aide memoire
Care practices which facilitate or restrict residents' scope to think or act independently

Written information
Information available from pre inspection questionnaire, plans, brochures and other documents seen before or during the inspection

Do care staff
- do things *with* or *for* people?
- spend time with residents?
- encourage residents to serve themselves or others at table?
- encourage them to make drinks/snacks?
- seek residents' views and wishes?
- act on residents wishes?
- perceive self-determination as an attribute or as 'difficult' behaviour?
- wear uniforms, and if so, does this create an expectation that people are there to be 'looked after'?
- operate a key worker system with duties promoting 'independence'.

Are there *'institutional' practices* which might restrict independence?
- Are bedrooms automatically cleaned without ascertaining residents' views?
- Is it *assumed* that residents will *not* hold pension book, handle other financial affairs, keep and administer their own medication, bathe themselves or carry out household tasks?

Are there *'implied' rules or accepted views* which restrict independence, say, about
- bedtimes?
- use of bedrooms, apart from at night?
- entertaining guests in bedrooms?

Do staff numbers and rotas allow
- time to help stimulate people? (it may be quicker to do things *for* them)
- resident contact time so as to ascertain their wishes and capabilities?

Are residents denied access to kitchen, laundry or other areas, and why?

General comment on matters not covered by these questions, and reactions/feelings of inspector which do not fit into the response columns above

Discussion

Information and comment from discussion with owner/manager, staff, residents and other people such as relatives and friends

Observation

Observations of inspector regarding attitudes, care practices, facilities, procedures, activities etc seen or heard during inspection

(Opportunities to think and act without reference to another person including a willingness to incur a degree of calculated risk.)

Aide memoire
Procedures or other arrangements set up to facilitate independence and monitor performance

Written information
Information available from pre inspection questionnaire, plans, brochures and other documents seen before or during the inspection

Do *case files* contain information about residents' physical and mental capabilities and the extent to which they wish or are able to act independently?
- Do files contain care plans?
- Who contributes to file information?
- Do files identify strengths/weaknesses?
- Do files identify aspects of race and culture which might be significant regarding attitudes to independence?
- Who has access to files?
- Do review reports cover independence?

Are records kept of cases where independence has to be *restricted by* staff in the interests of the person concerned or other parties? Are such cases regularly reviewed?

Is there a regular *review of policy*, procedures and care practices to monitor how they facilitate or restrict independence?
- Is it discussed at staff meetings?
- Is there an annual review/appraisal?

What procedures are there regarding people *going out*?
- Do residents have to seek permission?
- Do they have to inform staff?
- What are supervision arrangements regarding people who might be at risk when going out (eg EMD)?
- Do people have keys to the building?

Are residents involved in *discussions* about routine procedures/practices in the home, such as meal times or activities?

General comment on matters not covered by these questions, and reactions/feelings of inspector which do not fit into the response columns above

Discussion

Information and comment from discussion with owner/manager, staff, residents and other people such as relatives and friends

Observation

Observations of inspector regarding attitudes, care practices, facilities, procedures, activities etc seen or heard during inspection

(Opportunities to think and act without reference to another person including a willingness to incur a degree of calculated risk.)

Aide memoire
Extent to which *buildings, grounds, furniture or equipment* facilitate or restrict independence

Written information
Information available from pre inspection questionnaire, plans, brochures and other documents seen before or during the inspection

Do residents have their own *personal room* or space?
● Can they use it as they wish?
● Can they lock doors to room and cupboards?
● Can they control room temperature and lighting, open windows etc?
● Have they TV aerial, power supply and storage space?
● Is there space and furniture for entertaining guests?

Are there *facilities* for
● making drinks and snacks?
● washing personal laundry?
● making private telephone calls?

Are there adequate and appropriate *facilities and aids* aimed at reducing risks and helping to reduce loss of independence resulting from physical infirmity?
● Is the call system adequate and easy to operate?
● Are floors, steps and paths safe?
● Can lift be used unsupervised? Is it properly maintained?
● Are there aids to mobility for blind people?
● Are there aids to facilitate independent use of facilities (eg corridor handrails, grips in baths and wcs, bath seats etc)?
● Is equipment (eg kettles) regularly checked for safety?
● Are there different kinds of baths to suit different infirmities?

General comment on matters not covered by these questions, and reactions/feelings of inspector which do not fit into the response columns above

Discussion

Information and comment from discussion with owner/manager, staff, residents and other people such as relatives and friends

Observation

Observations of inspector regarding attitudes, care practices, facilities, procedures, activities etc seen or heard during inspection

(Opportunities to think and act without reference to another person including a willingness to incur a degree of calculated risk.)

Aide memoire	**Written information**
Extent to which *buildings, grounds, furniture and equipment* facilitate or restrict independence (continued)	Information available from pre inspection questionnaire, plans, brochures and other documents seen before or during the inspection

How *accessible and spacious* are
- bathrooms and wcs?
- facilities for private phone calls?
- all rooms and spaces for people with impaired mobility?

Are there *hazards* to inhibit mobility or make people wary of making their own way around the building, eg steep steps, poorly illuminated steps, slippery surfaces, holes in the carpet, raised thresholds or projections from walls such as lights or fire extinguishers?

How accessible are the *grounds* to people with poor mobility, sight or hearing? Are there hazards which inhibit movement?

How suitable is the home's *location* for access to shops, church, bank, post office etc

Are *furniture and furnishings* carefully chosen?
- Are beds too low for people to get from without help?
- Are chairs steady so that infirm people can use their support when getting up and so not need staff help?
- Is crockery of a size and design suitable for use by unsteady hands (eg tea pots)?
- Is equipment type (eg kettle, toaster) easy to use or lift/fill with water etc?
- Can curtains/blinds be closed or opened easily?
- Are floor coverings safe, non-slip etc?

General comment on matters not covered by these questions, and reactions/feelings of inspector which do not fit into the response columns above

Discussion

Information and comment from discussion with owner/manager, staff, residents and other people such as relatives and friends

Observation

Observations of inspector regarding attitudes, care practices, facilities, procedures, activities etc seen or heard during inspection

**The aide-memoire and
evaluation framework**

Name and address of home inspected
Date of visit
Name of inspector(s)
Name of inspecting agency

Suggested criteria for evaluation

The focus for this particular framework is CHOICE, which is defined as *'Opportunity to select independently from a range of options'*.

The suggested 'yardstick' against which performance (as indicted by the comment and information in the framework) should be measured is a notion of what a home which actively seeks to enable residents to exercise as much choice as possible about the content of their lives will be like. Such a 'good' home will seek to:—

1 recognise the inherent value to residents' well-being of their being able to exercise some choice about the content of their daily lives;

2 have a clear picture of residents' physical and mental capacities, and knowledge of the extent to which each person wishes and is able to make choices;

3 ensure that residents have adequate information on which to base decisions;

4 promote a care regime which facilitates and encourages residents to exercise choice regarding personal affairs, care and lifestyle in the context of an agreed notion of acceptable risk and constraints of communal life;

5 create a physical environment in which residents can choose to use a variety of spaces and facilities, and one which is safe from hazards and has aids for people with physical disabilities, so that inaccessibility or fear of accidents should not limit scope for exercising choice;

6 monitor each resident's condition and behaviour so as to ensure that a reasonable balance is achieved between self-determination, degree of risk involved, and impact on other people; and

7 create safeguards to ensure that any limitations placed on residents' right to exercise choice are explained, justified and reviewed regularly.

Furthermore, a 'good' home will have been selected from a range of options as an informed choice by the resident, with involvement of relatives and other advisers as appropriate to his or her ability to exercise choice.

NOTE FOR USERS When you have pursued your investigations into the home, using the aide memoire contained in the following pages, the findings you have recorded on the framework should be drawn on to produce an overall evaluation. Brief comments expressed in one or two sentences should be made in respect of each of the elements of a 'good' home outlined under 'Suggested criteria for evaluation', and there should be a general conclusion.

General conclusions

Aide Memoire

Extent to which residents' right to make informed choices about personal affairs, care and lifestyle in the context of an agreed notion of acceptable risk and constraints of communal life, is part of the home's *ethos*

Written information

Information available from pre inspection questionnaire, plans, brochures and other documents seen before or during the inspection

Does *owner/agency* recognise residents' right to exercise choice in
● brochure or other publicity?
● contracts with residents?
● day to day management?
● policy statements?

To what extent is there realisation that the safe and secure environment of the home should offer most residents *more* scope for choice than prior to admission?

Are there policy and guidelines about the degree of *risk taking* which is acceptable?

Do *staff* and *volunteers* understand that residents should be helped to exercise choice wherever possible?
● Have they a copy of the policy statement?
● Is it covered in induction training?
● Is it part of other training?
● Is it mentioned in records of training events?
● Is it discussed at recruitment interviews?
● Is it discussed at staff meetings? Is it in the minutes?
● Is it in job descriptions?
● Is it referred to in the staff manual?
● Have staff had formal training (eg CSS) which might help them appreciate importance of choice?

Do *residents and relatives* appear to understand residents' rights to exercise choice? Is any reference made in contracts, brochure or factsheet for potential and new residents?

General comments on matters not covered by these questions, and reactions/feelings of inspector which do not fit into the response columns above

Discussion

Information and comment from discussion with owner/manager, staff, residents and other people such as relatives and friends

Observation

Observations of inspector regarding attitudes, care practices, facilities, procedures, activities etc seen or heard during inspection

Aide Memoire

Care practices which facilitate or restrict residents' scope for choice, taking account of acceptable levels of risk

Written information

Information available from pre inspection questionnaire, plans, brochures and other documents seen before or during the inspection

Are there implied 'rules' or accepted views which *restrict* choice, say about
- use of bedrooms, apart from at night?
- 'entertaining' other residents or visitors in bedrooms?
- which lounges/dining rooms individuals must use?

Do residents in general have a say in selection of staff or rota planning?

Do individual residents have a say in
- who bathes/undresses them?
- who should be their key worker?

What is normal form of *personal address?*
How are decisions made about
- how residents should be addressed?
- how residents should address staff?

Do *staff numbers and rotas* allow for
- adequate resident contact time in which to get to know their wishes?
- staff to be available to help those requiring assistance with personal care to get up, have a bath or go to bed when they so wish?
- help to be provided for residents who wish to go out, say, to church?

Do *institutional practices* restrict choice?
- Do residents have their own clothing?
- Can they choose what to wear each day?
- Are there fixed bath times?
- Does laundry process reduce clothing choice?
- Are there fixed times for room cleaning?

General comments on matters not covered by these questions, and reactions/feelings of inspector which do not fit into the response columns above

Discussion

Information and comment from discussion with owner/manager, staff, residents and other people such as relatives and friends

Observation

Observations of inspector regarding attitudes, care practices, facilities, procedures, activities etc seen or heard during inspection

Aide Memoire

Procedures or other arrangements set up to facilitate the exercise of choice and to review performance

Written information

Information available from pre inspection questionnaire, plans, brochures and other documents seen before or during the inspection

What arrangements are there to provide *information and advice*, and opportunity for choosing GP, dentist, chiropodist or other professionals?
● Are lists supplied?
● Can residents retain their old GP if he or she is willing?
● Are residents advised on practicalities, say, of choosing someone living at a distance from the home to be their GP?
● Are details of charges available, where applicable?

Do *case files* contain information about residents' physical and mental capacities and the extent to which they wish or are able to make choices?

Do *case files* contain a care plan, or other record or residents' wishes regarding
● choice of GP etc?
● where to bank savings?
● choice of whether to handle personal financial affairs or personal medication?
● choice of funeral arrangements (eg name of church, cremation/burial, arrangements specific to minority religions and cultures etc?
● choice of will executor?

Are records kept in cases where choice has to be *restricted* by staff in the interests of the person concerned or other parties? Are such cases regularly reviewed?

General comments on matters not covered by these questions, and reactions/feelings of inspector which do not fit into the response columns above

Discussion

Information and comment from discussion with owner/manager, staff, residents and other people such as relatives and friends

Observation

Observations of inspector regarding attitudes, care practices, facilities, procedures, activities etc seen or heard during inspection

Aide Memoire

Procedures or other arrangements set up to facilitate the exercise of choice and to review performance (continued)

Written information

Information available from pre inspection questionnaire, plans, brochures and other documents seen before or during the inspection

---

Is there a regular *review of procedures* and care practices to monitor how they facilitate or restrict the range of choice open to residents?
- Is there an annual appraisal?
- Is it discussed in staff meetings or other forum?

Admission procedures
- Can people choose this home from a range of alternatives?
- What information are they given to assist choice?
- Can they stay for a short while before making a final decision?
- What can people bring with them, in terms of pets, furniture, personal possessions etc, and how are they made aware of this?
- Can new residents choose bedroom or resident group, within reason?

What happens when a resident decides to *move elsewhere*?
- Is there any degree of choice amongst local authority homes?
- Are lists of private or voluntary homes available, including accommodation charges?

General comments on matters not covered by these questions, and reactions/feelings of inspector which do not fit into the response columns above

Discussion

Information and comment from discussion with owner/manager, staff, residents and other people such as relatives and friends

Observation

Observations of inspector regarding attitudes, care practices, facilities, procedures, activities etc seen or heard during inspection

Aide Memoire
Choices regarding *meals and mealtimes*

Written information
Information available from pre inspection questionnaire, plans, brochures and other documents seen
before or during the inspection

What range of choice do residents have about
what they eat?
● Do menus offer a real choice, ie more than just,
  say, egg or cheese?
● Are diets catered for? (for health, religious or
  cultural reasons)
● Are vegetarians properly catered for?
● Is the home's capacity for offering choice
  unduly restricted by an inadequate budget?
● How easy is it in practice for someone to ask
  for something different?

Can residents choose *where* to eat?
● Can meals be delivered to bedrooms?
● Is there more than one dining space?
● Can they choose who to sit with?
● Can they avoid others with offensive habits?

Can residents decide *when* to eat?
● Is breakfast available over a substantial period
  so that people do not have to get up at fixed
  times?
● Are mealtimes fixed or can meals be kept hot
  for people going out or wishing to wait?
● Are there heated food trolleys so that, for
  instance, some groups can eat at different times
  than others?
● Can there be group decisions about mealtimes
  when going on outings?
● Can they make snacks/drinks when they wish,
  for themselves, friends or visitors?

Is scope for choice about what to eat, where and
when, restricted because staff are not available or
do not have enough time, as a result of *poorly
planned rotas* or *inadequate staff levels*? Do cooks
work flexible hours?

General comments on matters not covered by
these questions, and reactions/feelings of
inspector which do not fit into the response
columns above

Discussion

Information and comment from discussion with owner/manager, staff, residents and other people such as relatives and friends

Observation

Observations of inspector regarding attitudes, care practices, facilities, procedures, activities etc seen or heard during inspection

Aide Memoire
Extent to which *building and grounds* provide opportunities for choice

Written information
Information available from pre inspection questionnaire, plans, brochures and other documents seen before or during the inspection

Is there a range of *spaces, locations and facilities*
- to enable people of like minds to associate?
- to facilitate choice of peace/solitude or company?
- to enable people to get away from unwanted activities?
- to enable people to avoid smokers or TV?
- so that people can entertain guests?

Are *bedrooms* suitable for different uses?
- Can they be used as sitting rooms?
- Is there room to entertain guests?
- Are they furnished for resident and visitors?
- Can doors be locked?

What scope is there for residents to choose, in bedroom and elsewhere
- furniture, curtains, carpets etc?
- decor?
- room temperature, whether to have light on or window open etc?

Are there adequate and appropriate *aids and adaptations* so as to help ensure that physical infirmity does not result in undue restriction of choice?
- Is there a lift so that people are not restricted to one floor?
- Are floors, steps and paths safe?
- Are there aids to help blind people find their way?
- Do aids/adaptations enable people to choose, say, when to get out of bed, or when to bathe, when staff would otherwise be required?
- Is the call system easy to use?

General comments on matters not covered by these questions, and reactions/feelings of inspector which do not fit into the response columns above

Discussion

Information and comment from discussion with owner/manager, staff, residents and other people such as relatives and friends

Observation

Observations of inspector regarding attitudes, care practices, facilities, procedures, activities etc seen or heard during inspection

Rights

The aide-memoire and evaluation framework

Name and address of home inspected
Date of visit
Name of inspector(s)
Name of inspecting agency

Suggested criteria for evaluation

The focus for this particular framework is the safeguarding of HUMAN RIGHTS, defined as *'The maintenance of all entitlements associated with citizenship'*. The criteria are derived from the Human Rights Convention 1950, adapted as necessary to relate to residential care.

The suggested 'yardstick' against which performance (as indicated by comment and information in the framework) should be measured, is a notion of what a home which pays due regard to residents' rights will be like. Such a 'good' home will seek to:—

1 ensure that residents are not subjected to inhuman or degrading treatment, whether physical or mental, or compelled to undertake domestic or other tasks against their will;
2 encourage freedom of conscience, thought and religion, and facilitate participation in the political process and in chosen activities, religious or otherwise;
3 encourage freedom of expression, meaning the right to complain, to hold opinions, and to receive and impart information and ideas, particularly regarding personal care and treatment;
4 maintain the right to liberty, including from participation in care and treatment;
5 respect private and family life, confidentiality of personal affairs, and personal space;
6 permit and facilitate chosen personal relationships, sexual or otherwise and including marriage, between residents and between residents and other acquaintances;
7 permit and facilitate opportunities for social and other gatherings for whatever purpose inside and outwith the home, and place no restrictions on participation;
8 supply information to residents and apply appropriate types and levels of support to encourage and enable them to exercise their rights;
9 safeguard individual rights without discriminating on any grounds, whether gender, age, race, colour, language, religion or other status, or political or other opinion;
10 ensure that where it is deemed necessary to interfere with or restrict an individual's rights for the protection of that person or the rights and freedoms of others, or for any other reasons, such actions are recorded, explained to the individual and other interested parties and reviewed regularly according to an agreed procedure; and
11 have mechanisms for monitoring the home's performance in safeguarding residents' rights.

NOTE FOR USERS When you have pursued your investigations into the home, using the aide memoire contained in the following pages, the findings you have recorded on the framework should be drawn on to produce an overall evaluation. Brief comments expressed in one or two sentences should be made in respect of each of the elements of a 'good' home outlined under 'Suggested criteria for evaluation', and there should be a general conclusion.

General conclusions

Aide Memoire
Extent to which respect for human rights is part of the *home's ethos*

Written information
Information available from pre inspection question-naire, plans, brochures and other documents seen before or during the inspection

Does *owner/agency* recognise rights
- in brochure or other publicity?
- in contracts with residents?
- in day to day management?
- in policy statements?

Do *staff understand* about human rights and that admission to a home does not imply any reduction of such rights?
- Is it covered in induction training?
- Is it part of other training?
- Is it mentioned in records of training events?
- Is it discussed at recruitment interviews?
- Is it discussed at staff meetings? Is it mentioned in minutes?
- Is it in job descriptions?
- Is it referred to in the staff manual?
- Have staff had formal training (eg CSS) which might help them appreciate importance of safeguarding rights?

Do *residents and relatives* appear to understand their rights? Is any reference made in
- a fact sheet for potential and new residents?
- contracts or brochures?
What are people told before admission?

What efforts are made to see that *volunteers* or people on *special schemes* (eg ET) understand residents rights
- in training?
- in contracts of employment?
- in supervision?

General comments on matters not covered by these questions, and reactions/feelings of inspector which do not fit into the response columns above

Discussion

Information and comment from discussion with owner/manager, staff, residents and other people such as relatives and friends

Observation

Observations of inspector regarding attitudes, care practices, facilities, procedures, activities etc seen or heard during inspection

Aide Memoire
Extent to which *care practice* recognises and
safeguards residents' rights

Written information
Information available from pre inspection questionnaire, plans, brochures and other documents seen
before or during the inspection

How are residents involved in *decisions* about
their care or treatment, and how they occupy their
time
- before admission decision is taken?
- during admission process?
- in daily contact?
- in reviews?

How are residents encouraged and helped to *vote*
in elections?
- Are they all on the electoral register?
- Do they receive voting cards?
- Do they have help with transport?
- Where necessary, are they helped with reading
  and marking ballot forms?
- How are they protected from undue influence
  by others as to who to support?

How are residents encouraged and helped to
follow chosen *religious worship or other activities*,
or to maintain contact with relatives and friends?
- By arranging transport?
- Welcoming visitors?
- Contacts with Churches and other
  organisations?

What is the general *atmosphere*?
- Do relationships between residents, and
  between residents and staff appear friendly and
  open?
- Do residents feel able to say what they think?
- Do residents or staff appear 'cowed' or
  subdued?
- Do staff spend time with residents?

General comments on matters not covered by
these questions, and reactions/feelings of
inspector which do not fit into the response
columns above

Discussion

Information and comment from discussion with owner/manager, staff, residents and other people such as relatives and friends

Observation

Observations of inspector regarding attitudes, care practices, facilities, procedures, activities etc seen or heard during inspection

Aide Memoire
Extent to which *care practice* recognises and safeguards residents' rights (continued)

Written information
Information available from pre inspection questionnaire, plans, brochures and other documents seen before or during the inspection

What efforts are made to *facilitate residents' control over* who to associate with?
- Allocation to bedroom, living or dining room.
- Allocation of tables in dining room.
- Freedom of movement, within and outwith the home.
- Privacy of personal space.

How *sensitively* do staff handle situations where exercise of individual rights affects the rights and freedoms of others, for example
- where behaviour is offensive to others?
- where one person 'dominates' or frightens others?

Is there suspicion or evidence of *restriction of liberty, or inhuman/degrading treatment*?
- In staff attitudes?
- In observed daily routines?
- In records or case files?
- In admission procedures?
- Are residents coerced by staff into engaging in activities, eating meals, going to bed at certain times etc?
- Are residents ever struck or forcibly restrained?
- Are residents forced to work against their will?
- Have residents access to a private telephone?
- Is there any restriction on sending or receiving mail?
- Are doors locked unnecessarily?
- Are surveillance cameras used?
- Do bedroom doors have windows or spyholes?

General comments on matters not covered by these questions, and reactions/feelings of inspector which do not fit into the response columns above

Discussion

Information and comment from discussion with owner/manager, staff, residents and other people such as relatives and friends

Observation

Observations of inspector regarding attitudes, care practices, facilities, procedures, activities etc seen or heard during inspection

Aide Memoire
Extent to which *care practice* recognises and safeguards residents' rights (continued)

Written information
Information available from pre inspection questionnaire, plans, brochures and other documents seen before or during the inspection

Is there suspicion or evidence that rights *are restricted* on grounds of gender, age, colour, language, religion or other status, or political or other opinion:—
- in range of activities available?
- in menus?
- in the way staff treat residents?
- in records or case files?

Handling of *residents' personal affairs*
- What is policy regarding control over personal finances?
- How are residents/relatives/advisers consulted?
- How are decisions made for owner/manager to handle residents' personal finances? Are they recorded?
- Are decisions routinely reviewed?

What arrangements are there for *staff* to approach owner/manager *in confidence* when aware of ill treatment or unsanctioned restriction of rights?

General comments on matters not covered by these questions, and reactions/feelings of inspector which do not fit into the response columns above

Discussion

Information and comment from discussion with owner/manager, staff, residents and other people such as relatives and friends

Observation

Observations of inspector regarding attitudes, care practices, facilities, procedures, activities etc seen or heard during inspection

Aide Memoire
Procedures intended to help safeguard the rights of individuals and residents in general

Written information
Information available from pre inspection questionnaire, plans, brochures and other documents seen before or during the inspection

Is there a *written complaints* procedure?
- Is it prominently displayed?
- Are residents, relatives/advisers and staff aware of it?
- Does it specify who to complain to
  - within the home?
  - within the organisation owning/managing the home?
  - outwith the home (eg Councillor, MP, Ombudsman)
- Is there a record of complaints made and action taken in response?
- Is it used? How often?

Where residents' *rights are restricted*, what are the procedures for—
- recording such actions?
- explaining and justifying decisions to residents/advisers?
- notifying owner, managing agency or registration authority?
- reviewing such decisions?

Is there a policy about residents' *access to personal files*
- If so, what is it? Is it written down and communicated to residents and relatives/advisers?
- If not, what happens in practice?

Is there a mechanism for *reviewing* the home's performance in safeguarding rights of residents in general:—
- by way of annual review, staff meeting or staff evaluation process?
- by examining effect of institutional practices on rights?

General comments on matters not covered by these questions, and reactions/feelings of inspector which do not fit into the response columns above

Discussion

Information and comment from discussion with owner/manager, staff, residents and other people such as relatives and friends

Observation

Observations of inspector regarding attitudes, care practices, facilities, procedures, activities etc seen or heard during inspection

Fulfilment

**The aide-memoire and
evaluation framework**

Name and address of home inspected
Date of visit
Name of inspector(s)
Name of inspecting agency

Suggested criteria for evaluation

The focus of this particular framework is FULFILMENT, which is defined as *'The realisation of personal aspirations and abilities in all aspects of daily life'*.

The suggested 'yardstick' against which performance (as indicated by the comment and information in the framework) should be measured, is a notion of what a home which actively helps residents to lead fulfilling lives will be like. Such a 'good' home will seek to:—

1 know of some of the things that residents have done in earlier life, and the skills and interests which they retain;
2 help residents to continue to use such skills and follow such interests, if they so wish, and to aspire to new ones;
3 foster the maintenance of established personal relationships and create conditions which facilitate the development of new ones, where so desired;
4 build on residents' positive features, such as experience and knowledge, rather than merely 'manage' negative features such as confusion or physical incapacity;
5 help residents to use their physical and mental faculties, within the limit of their abilities and wishes, but recognise and cater for those who have no wish to be active or sociable;
6 understand and cater for the emotional and spiritual needs of residents;
7 encourage and enable residents to participate in making decisions about their own lifestyle insofar as they are willing and able to do so;
8 create a stimulating environment and provide appropriate supporting services; and
9 create a lifestyle which is flexible and which can adapt and develop as residents change.

NOTE FOR USERS When you have pursued your investigations into the home, using the aide memoire contained in the following pages, the findings you have recorded on the framework should be drawn on to produce an overall evaluation. Brief comments expressed in one or two sentences should be made in respect of each of the elements of a 'good' home outlined under 'Suggested criteria for evaluation', and there should be a general conclusion.

General conclusions

Aide memoire

Understanding of *concept of fulfilment* and role of residential care in providing appropriate opportunities and stimulation.

Written information

Information available from pre inspection questionnaire, plans, brochures and other documents seen before or during the inspection

---

Does the owner/agency *promote fulfilment* as a major objective of the home
- in brochure, fact sheet or other publicity material?
- in day to day management?

Do staff understand the desirability of encouraging and enabling residents to maximise potential? Do staff appreciate that homes should widen the range of opportunities open to residents?
- Is it included in induction training?
- Is it included in in-service training?
- Is it discussed at staff meetings?
- Is it part of job descriptions?
- Is it referred to in staff manual?
- Have staff undergone formal training such as CSS which would help them appreciate the importance of maximising potential?

Do staff understand that fulfilment of potential can be hindered by *practices geared to administrative convenience*? (eg carrying out tasks such as bed-making without regard to residents' need or wishes).

Do *volunteers* have any understanding of the concept of fulfilment?
- Do they have any training?
- Do they have specified duties?

Do residents and relatives understand that admission to a home should *not* mean diminution in opportunity, but rather the opposite?
- Is there a fact sheet for potential residents?
- What are they told before admission?
- What does brochure say?
- Does contract say anything?

General comment on matters not covered by these questions, and reactions/feelings of inspector which do not fit into the response columns above.

Discussion

Information and comment from discussion with owner/manager, staff, residents and other people such as relatives and friends

Observation

Observations of inspector regarding attitudes, care practices, facilities, procedures, activities etc seen or heard during inspection

(The realisation of personal aspirations and abilities in all aspects of daily life)

Aide memoire

Efforts made *to plan to meet the needs of residents* and to ensure that their wishes and aspirations are known

Written information

Information available from pre inspection questionnaire, plans brochures and other documents seen before or during the inspection

Is there a *written care plan* for each resident?
If Yes:
● Are residents, relatives, advisers involved?
● Do they include plans for maximising potential?
● Do they identify strengths/weaknesses?
● Do they specify involvement of relatives, friends, volunteers or personal advisers?
● Do they take account of race/culture/class/sex?
● Do they include measures to ensure that physical needs are reviewed and catered for (eg provision of aids)?
● Do they take account of spiritual and emotional needs of residents?
● Who is involved in reviews?

In practice, do written care plans mean anything?
● Are plans pursued with enthusiasm?
● Is progress reviewed? If so how often?

If there are no written care plans, is there *any other evidence* that efforts are made to plan for individuals or groups?
● Do case records say anything?
● Are there any references in the daily diary/occurrence book?
● Do staff discuss matters with residents and relatives, friends etc, where appropriate (bearing in mind question of confidentiality)?

In written or other care plans, what account is taken of clients who may *not* wish to do anything?

Do plans take account of the need to safeguard rights of residents?

General comment on matters not covered by these questions, and reactions/feelings of inspector which do not fit into the response columns above

Discussion

Information and comment from discussion with owner/manager, staff, residents and other people such as relatives and friends

Observation

Observations of inspector regarding attitudes, care practices, facilities, procedures, activities etc seen or heard during inspection

FORM **F** **FULFILMENT**

(The realisation of personal aspirations and abilities in all aspects of daily life)

Aide memoire

Efforts made by management and staff to *encourage/help/stimulate* residents to maximise potential

Written information

Information available from pre inspection questionnaire, plans brochures and other documents seen before or during the inspection

Are things done *with*, rather than for, residents?

How are residents *encouraged/stimulated/*helped to do such things as:—
- chose furniture/furnishings/decoration?
- helping to tidy up their bedroom?
- helping with other chores?
- planning, preparing or serving meals?
- planning entertainment/activities?

What mechanisms are there for residents and staff *to plan things together*?
- Is there a residents' committee?
- If so, are there agendas and minutes?

Do staff have *time* to offer help/stimulation? Are *numbers* adequate?

Is there *continuity* of contact between staff and residents?
- Key worker or similar system?
- Do rotas take continuity into account?
- Is staff turnover excessive?

Does recruitment and interviewing process take account of need to recruit staff with an interest in providing help/stimulation?

Are efforts made to acquire *materials* for activities, (eg knitting wool or books)?

Do staff respect the *wishes of residents* who prefer to do nothing?

What efforts are made to ensure that residents *can go out of the home*, say, to Church, to visit friends or to vote in elections?

General comment on matters not covered by these questions, and reactions/feelings of inspector which do not fit into the response columns above.

Discussion

Information and comment from discussion with owner/manager, staff, residents and other people such as relatives and friends

Observation

Observations of inspector regarding attitudes, care practices, facilities, procedures, activities etc seen or heard during inspection

Aide memoire
Suitability of *building and grounds* in terms of location, facilities, accessibility, safety and security

Written information
Information available from pre inspection questionnaire, plans brochures and other documents seen before or during the inspection

Is the *location* of the home suitable in terms of easy access to facilities (eg bank, shops, pub, post office, transport)?

Do the building and grounds provide a *safe, secure and manageable* environment in which residents can be active?
- En suite facilities in bedrooms?
- Can doors/cupboard doors be locked?
- Are bedroom facilities accessible? (eg cupboards, wardrobes, wash basins)
- Are toilets and bathrooms accessible?
- Are there adequate and appropriate aids/adaptations to facilitate self help and movement around the building and grounds (eg rails, lifts)?
- Are there hazards to inhibit activity? (eg steep steps, badly illuminated steps, slippery surfaces, holes in carpet, raised thresholds, or projections from walls, such as lights or fire extinguishers)
- Are security arrangements satisfactory?

What arrangements are there to *review conditions* and update where necessary?

Are there facilities and equipment suitable for self-help activities (eg for making drinks or doing personal laundry)?

Are facilities and space adequate and suitable for *activities*, (eg education, crafts/hobbies, occupational therapy, gardening, beauty care or any other special interests)?

Are facilities appropriate for entertaining *visitors*?
- Is there a private place to meet?
- Are there facilities for refreshments?

General comment on matters not covered by these questions, and reactions/feelings of inspector which do not fit into the response columns above.

Discussion

Information and comment from discussion with owner/manager, staff, residents and other people such as relatives and friends

Observation

Observations of inspector regarding attitudes, care practices, facilities, procedures, activities etc seen or heard during inspection

Aide Memoire

Availability of health care and other support services to enable residents to be active within the limits of their wishes and abilities

Written Information

Information available from pre inspection questionnaire, plans brochures and other documents seen before or during the inspection

Are *supportive services* available?
- Library service. Does it cater for ethnic minorities (languages/authors)?
- College of further education
- Occupational therapist
- Hairdressing for those who cannot go out or who have special needs (eg Afro-Caribbean people)
- Do clergy visit (eg Vicar, Rabbi etc)

Are *arrangements for health* care adequate and appropriate so that residents' capacity for activity is known and monitored?
- Access to physiotherapy treatment?
- Consultations with GP or consultant in respect of both physical and mental conditions?
- Are district nurses available?
- Is there a regular chiropody service?
- Are there adequate arrangements for testing hearing and eyesight?
- Are there arrangements for routine dental examination, treatment, renewal of dentures etc?

Are *relatives, friends, neighbours* or personal advisers made welcome?

Are *volunteers* used to help residents engage in activities, to befriend and support them or take them out to shops, bank, theatre etc?

Is there any *social work* support available for the home or for individual residents?

Does the home provide any *transport* for residents?

General comment on matters not covered by these questions, and reactions/feelings of inspector which do not fit into the response columns above

Discussion

Information and comment from discussion with owner/manager, staff, residents and other people such as relatives and friends

Observation

Observations of inspector regarding attitudes, care practices, facilities, procedures, activities etc seen or heard during inspection

CHAPTER 5

The written report

A suggested approach to report writing based on the pre-inspection questionnaire (Chapter 3) and the aide memoire and evaluation framework (Chapter 4)

Introduction

This evaluation model is suitable for use by all those with an interest in residential care of elderly people, whether they be owners, managers, practitioners, trainers, inspectors or perhaps service consumers. When it is used for inspections a final essential element is the written report. This is important not only for the inspection agency, but also as a means of informing those subject to inspections of judgements made about their work and to identify areas of potential improvement.

The form of such a report, and the procedure for sharing it with those concerned is, of course, up to each agency to decide. However, the following format has been successfully used for reporting on inspections based on the pre-inspection questionnaire and the framework for evaluation contained in this model.

The format is based on the sections of those two forms. It merely lists headings, together with suggestions of what might be covered under each one, and indicates a need for a summary and recommendations.

The written report

1. **Introduction**
   Reason for inspection, method used etc

2. **Basic information**
   Nature of establishment, stated function, registration etc

3. **Residents**
   Occupancy, admissions and discharges, contact with relatives and friends, dependency, case files, contracts, complaints etc

4. **Finance**
   Charges, pension arrangements, personal finances, purchase of clothing etc

5. **Premises**
   General description, decor and condition, comfort, privacy and association, visitors, safety, fire, environmental health etc

6. **Care, social development and management**
   Assessment and review, staff roles, social and emotional development, meals, mealtimes, health etc

7. **Organisation, management and staff**
   Staff structure, job descriptions, supervision, age, gender, ethnicity, qualifications, training, stability, administration etc

8. **Records**
   The home and the individual

9. **Quality of residential experience**
   Privacy, dignity, independence, choice, rights and fulfilment
   (In the case of each of these, content might be directly related to the criteria of what a 'good' home would seek to achieve).

10. **Summary and recommendations**

11. **Appendices**
    For example, plan of building, client dependency rating survey, brochure etc

Printed in the United Kingdom for HMSO
Dd302139 2/96 C30 G3397 10170